First published in Great Britain in 2000 by
David & Charles Children's Books,
Winchester House, 259-269 Old Marylebone Road, London NW1 5XJ

Text © Adèle Geras 2000
Illustrations © Emma Chichester Clark 2000

The rights of Adèle Geras and Emma Chichester Clark to be identified as the author
and illustrator of this work have been asserted by them in accordance with the
Copyright, Designs and Patents Act, 1988.

ISBN: 1 86233 226 6

A CIP catalogue record for this title is available from the British Library.

Printed and bound in Belgium

The Magic of the Ballet

Giselle

RETOLD BY ADÈLE GERAS

ILLUSTRATED BY EMMA CHICHESTER CLARK

David & Charles
Children's Books

The Magic of the Ballet

HUMAN BEINGS LIKE TO move their bodies in time to rhythm. Even the tiniest babies enjoy being rocked or gently bounced as you sing to them, and we all know how feet long to move when we hear a strong and exciting beat. "That's toe-tapping music," we say, and what we mean is we would like to dance to it.

There are many different kinds of dance: folk, disco, ballroom, tap and so on.

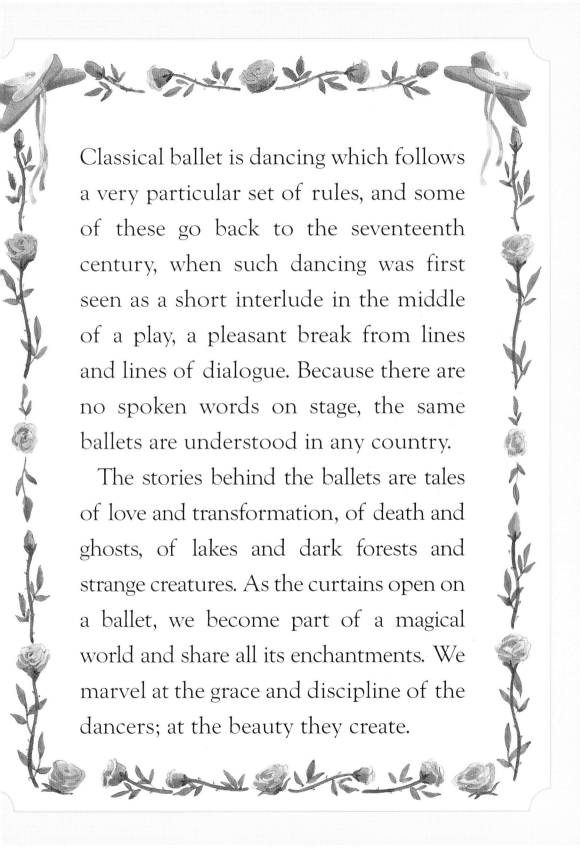

Classical ballet is dancing which follows a very particular set of rules, and some of these go back to the seventeenth century, when such dancing was first seen as a short interlude in the middle of a play, a pleasant break from lines and lines of dialogue. Because there are no spoken words on stage, the same ballets are understood in any country.

The stories behind the ballets are tales of love and transformation, of death and ghosts, of lakes and dark forests and strange creatures. As the curtains open on a ballet, we become part of a magical world and share all its enchantments. We marvel at the grace and discipline of the dancers; at the beauty they create.

'It was Giselle's voice, and I was filled with
a happiness I thought was lost forever.'

Giselle

EVERYTHING THEY SAY ABOUT old age is true. I find that I remember in the clearest detail everything that happened to me in my youth, and yet I would have difficulty in telling you what I ate this morning when I awoke.

Sometimes I forget how quickly the years have gone by and when I catch sight of myself in the glass, I do not recognize the white-haired, old man I see. This cannot be me, Albrecht. Albrecht was tall and straight. He had clear blue eyes and a smiling mouth. And he was loved, oh yes indeed. I may have forgotten many things, but the memory of Giselle's love for me still remains. I think of her every day, and there is a small, vain part of my soul that rejoices to think she never saw me as an old man. To her I am still young.

Giselle lived in the village of . . . but no, the name has gone. No matter. It was a collection of small, well-kept cottages that clung to the side of a hill where the forest ended.

I was hiding in this village, I confess it. I had become bored with palace life, with ceremony, with decorum, and all I wanted that spring was to roam through the woods like a peasant, hunting when it suited me.

It wasn't really even Bathilde I was escaping from. Our families had arranged that we would be married. Bathilde was considered to be a beauty and her father was the Duke of Courland. My parents persuaded me it would be a splendid alliance, and I reluctantly agreed. My flight to the village was a last chance for the kind of freedom I knew I could never have as a married man, nor as the future Duke of Silesia.

If it were not for Giselle, I should probably have returned to the palace within days, but once I caught sight of her, everything else in my life shrank away and I never gave the palace or my duty a single thought. I found a cottage and paid the owner money to rent it, and I took the name of Loys.

How can I find words to describe Giselle? I loved her from the very first moment I laid eyes on her, and she loved me too. She was pale. Her hair was like ravens' feathers. She danced for happiness, but there was always something fragile about her. I don't know how to put it more accurately. Always I had the thought in my mind when we were together, 'be careful, oh, be careful,' for I knew she could so easily be hurt.

Hilarion, the young gamekeeper in the village, adored Giselle too. He could see that Giselle and I loved each other, and his jealousy grew and grew.

On the morning of the harvest feast, I came very near to telling Giselle who I really was.

She had been teasing me, asking me why it was that I was different from other men she had known, and begging me to tell her where I had come from and who my family were.

"It doesn't matter," I answered. "You are my family, my whole world. You are the one I love."

"Oh, but do you? Do you truly? Let this flower tell us." She picked a late rose and began idly to pluck the petals from it. "He loves me, he loves me not . . . "
"Will you believe a flower that knows nothing of how I feel? Will you not believe me?"

Suddenly I was filled with dread at what Giselle would do if the last petal fell on 'he loves me not'. How relieved I was then, to pull the last petal from the stem.

"I love you! You see? Even this rose knows this is the truth!" I cried.

Giselle smiled, happy for the moment.

"Go with the others, Loys, to gather the last of the harvest, and I will stay here and prepare the feast," she said.

And I went. I went gladly. I thought myself the most fortunate man alive, striding away with the others into the valley while the September sun shone all around us, as golden and sparkling as the wine we would soon be enjoying. Try to imagine my joy as a bubble, and look at it now, catching the light. Soon it will burst, and neither I nor anyone else will ever lay eyes on it again.

Much later, during that long, infinitely black night while we watched over Giselle's body before her funeral, her weeping mother told me what had happened. I hear her words even now, half a lifetime later. I still wonder if there was anything I could have done differently that

would have prevented Giselle's dreadful end.

"We heard the horns, and the hounds baying," her mother told me, "and soon a hunting-party arrived in the village. Everyone gathered round, for we had never seen such grand people. Princess Bathilde was the most splendid of all, in a gown the colour of a dark red rose. Everyone was falling over themselves to offer hospitality. Giselle helped to serve the wine, and Princess Bathilde was struck with her beauty and grace."

Here Giselle's mother paused and wiped the tears from her eyes. "Bathilde asked my poor daughter question after question. She begged her to come to the palace as her own serving-lady, but when she found out that Giselle was in love and soon to be married, she smiled kindly.

'It is my loss,' she said, 'and you shall have my own necklace as a wedding-gift.'

She fastened a chain of gold filigree around Giselle's neck and my daughter danced away to

show the wonderful present to all her friends. The royal party came into my house to rest

before their homeward journey, and then you came back from the vineyards and the festival began. My daughter had been chosen as the Queen of the Harvest. How joyously she danced! Do you remember? Oh, oh, I cannot bear to think of what has happened!"

And I, even though I cannot bear it, am condemned to turn it over constantly in my mind. I remember how we danced, and then

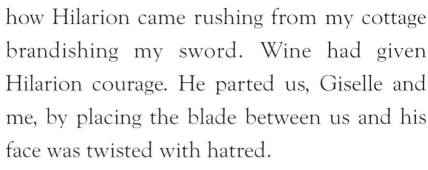

how Hilarion came rushing from my cottage brandishing my sword. Wine had given Hilarion courage. He parted us, Giselle and me, by placing the blade between us and his face was twisted with hatred.

"You are the son of the Duke of Silesia, and not Loys at all. I have the proof." He turned to the villagers. "He brought too many possessions with him for a humble peasant. He has deceived us, and he has bewitched you, Giselle, with his false promises."

The royal party came out of Giselle's cottage to see what all the shouting was about, and Bathilde caught sight of me at once.

"Albrecht!" she cried, "What are you doing here among these simple folk?" She ran to my side and said, "See, Giselle, I too have my betrothed. This is Albrecht, and I hope that you will be as happy in your marriage as we in ours." And each word was like a dagger in my poor Giselle's heart! Giselle turned to me.

"Please say that she is lying, Loys," she whispered. My mouth was full of ashes, and my heart was as cold as a stone in my body. I could say nothing.

Do you believe that someone can die of a broken heart? I had thought it was a fanciful notion, invented by lovesick poets, but that was before Giselle's death.

She tore at the necklace Bathilde had given her and it snapped as though it were no more than a thin string of silk. Then she took my jewelled sword from Hilarion and plunged it into her side. How could he have let her take it? How could he have prevented her? She had the strength of despair in her hands. Still, it was not the wound that killed her. I did. I killed her as surely as though I had squeezed the life out of her with my own hands. She danced like a marionette with broken strings. She danced like a doll with no life left in her. Her soul flew out of her

before our eyes. The anguish in her heart drove all reason from her and she fell at last into her mother's arms.

The feast was over. No one moved for a long time. Then Bathilde's party left the village. There was nothing they could do. No one was interested in them any longer. We were numb with grief, all of us, and hardly noticed the departure. There was nothing left for us to do but mourn.

"I should throw you from this house," said Giselle's mother, "but my daughter loved you." That was how I came to watch all night over Giselle's body, until her funeral the next day.

Do you believe in Wilis? They are the spirits of young girls who have died before their wedding day, deceived by their lovers, tricked by lies. There were tales told about them by country people. It was said they appeared at midnight, on the swampy shores of a hidden lake, led by their queen, Myrtha, who was tall and white and merciless. The Wilis danced till the first light of dawn, and as the sun's rays touched them, they dissolved, every one of them, into thin mists, stretching and curling and hovering over the water. If an unfortunate young man were to meet one of them in the dark, he would be enchanted by her beauty and she would dance with him, in and out of the black trees in the moonlight, and her white, white arms would wind themselves like smoke

around his neck, and she would call to her sisters and together they would follow and follow the dance, until there was no more strength in him and he breathed his last.

Everyone warned me. "Do not go to Giselle's grave at night. Some say she is now one of Queen Myrtha's misty maidens, and she will dance you to your death."

But I thought, 'If I could see Giselle again, I would gladly pay with my life.' So I said only, "There are flowers I must lay on her grave. Do not try to prevent me."

I knew that there was no one brave enough to stop me as I made my way to where she lay buried.

I threw myself down near the wooden cross carved with Giselle's name. I was beside myself with grief. Then I saw Hilarion slipping through the trees. Could he have arrived before me? The thought flew in and out of my mind like a butterfly and waves of sorrow overwhelmed me.

I laid my face on the cold earth.

"My darling," said a voice near me, and I

knew it. It was Giselle's voice, and I was filled with a happiness I thought was lost forever. I looked up, and the blood froze in my veins. It was indeed Giselle and yet she was transformed. Her eyes were like black pools and her mouth was a bloodstain in her chalk-white face.

"Go, my love," she whispered. "I cannot protect you from your fate if you remain here. They . . . we will surely lead you to your grim death. Come quickly with me and I will endeavour to hide you."

I followed her into the darkness between the trees, but at that moment we saw Hilarion dancing with the white maidens. I watched him, pulled this way and that like something blown by the wind, or pulled by the tides, until at last he sank into the waters of the black lake whose surface glittered in the moonlight.

"Look," Giselle whispered. "Our Queen approaches." Queen Myrtha towered over her maidens. Her face was a mask and her dress moved around her like a cloud.

"There is a stranger in our midst," she said. "I can smell him. Giselle, where have you hidden him, the man who drove you to your death? Bring him out to us. We wish for him to dance with us."

Giselle turned to me. "Hold tightly to the cross on my grave," she said. "It is the only thing that will protect you. Do not let go.

Whatever happens, hold tightly onto the cross. I will plead with our Queen. Perhaps she will be merciful."

Giselle begged for my life, but Queen Myrtha was unmoved.

"He will dance," she said, "like all the others. He will dance until he can dance no longer. Go to him."

At first, I shut my eyes and clung to the cross, but I couldn't bear not to see my beloved when she was so close to me.

"Turn away," she cried. "Hold fast."

But I could not. I had to hold her in my arms once more. I had to dance with her, even if death was the punishment.

"No," she whispered. "How will I protect you if they come . . . all my pale sisters?"

And of course they did come, all the ghostly dancers, pulling me here and there, making me feel dizzy and sick.

"Do not fall, my love," Giselle said to me as

we whirled and turned. "Lean on me. I will carry you. Do not lose heart. The light of dawn will soon be here."

As we danced, I lost all thought of where I was and yet I knew that the Wilis were drawing me nearer and nearer to the water. Sometimes I caught sight of it among the trees, but only for an instant, so frantic was the dance. I could feel Giselle breathing cold words of love in my ear.

"Come with me. The dawn is nearly here."

Blindly, nearly exhausted, I followed her. We were very near her grave. I could see the cross I should have clung to, and my own flowers beside it. Then, I caught sight of the sky above the trees. Day was breaking.

"Thank the Lord," Giselle said, "for another dawn. They cannot touch you now. Look."

The Wilis were melting in the light. Even their queen was blurring at the edges and fading away among the trees.

"Stay," I groaned. "Do not leave me here alone, Giselle. What will I do but weep for you?"

"Then weep you shall," she sighed, "for I must return to the grave."

Her shape was disappearing into the earth. Before I could say another word, she was gone. She had saved me with her love and condemned me to a lifetime of remorse and sorrow.

That life is now nearly at an end. I pray that beyond the grave I will be reunited with Giselle. I pray for that.

GISELLE WAS FIRST PERFORMED at the Paris Opéra in 1841. It was choreographed by Jean Coralli for the ballerina Carlotta Grisi. The French poet, Théophile Gautier, devised the story from a German original by fellow poet, Heinrich Heine. The music is by Adolphe Adam. Giselle is a wonderful part for any female dancer, a part she dreams of throughout her long and difficult training.

Of all the arts, ballet is probably the most demanding. Not everyone has the right frame, strength or temperament to be trained as a dancer. Those who do must have a passion for ballet and the discipline that goes with it. They must be ready for the hardest possible work, and many setbacks and disappointments.

All dancers have to devote themselves to their training, which begins in early childhood and never ends, however famous they become. Even the greatest principal dancers have to attend class daily, doing many of the same exercises as the youngest beginner, in order to maintain the strength and suppleness of their bodies. Dancers must try to avoid injury, and this is why the daily class is so important: it is much easier to damage limbs that have not been thoroughly stretched and warmed-up.

The names given to the steps and exercises are in French, and wherever you learn to dance, you will use the same terms. Five foot positions must be learned, and each jump, turn and lift has its own name which is known to every dancer.

In many ballets, the ballerina in particular takes on the form of a bird, a ghost, or a fairy, and weightlessness is part of the illusion being created. Lightness and grace have always been two of the main qualities of a ballerina. Thanks to more sophisticated training techniques, dancers today are much more athletic than they used to be. Eating enough food to give strength without putting on too much weight is a constant preoccupation for the ballet dancer. It is vital that young dancers eat a well-balanced diet during the years that their bodies are developing. They should never try to lose weight by cutting down on their food intake.

It used to be thought unmanly for boys to show an interest in ballet-dancing, but anyone who sees a video of Irek Mukhamedov or Tetsuya Kumakawa will know that a dancer requires all the power and energy we associate with the strongest athletes.

Many of the greatest dancers eventually become teachers. In this way, they pass on steps and stylistic techniques which would otherwise disappear, and the dancers of today become part of a long tradition of beauty and precision.

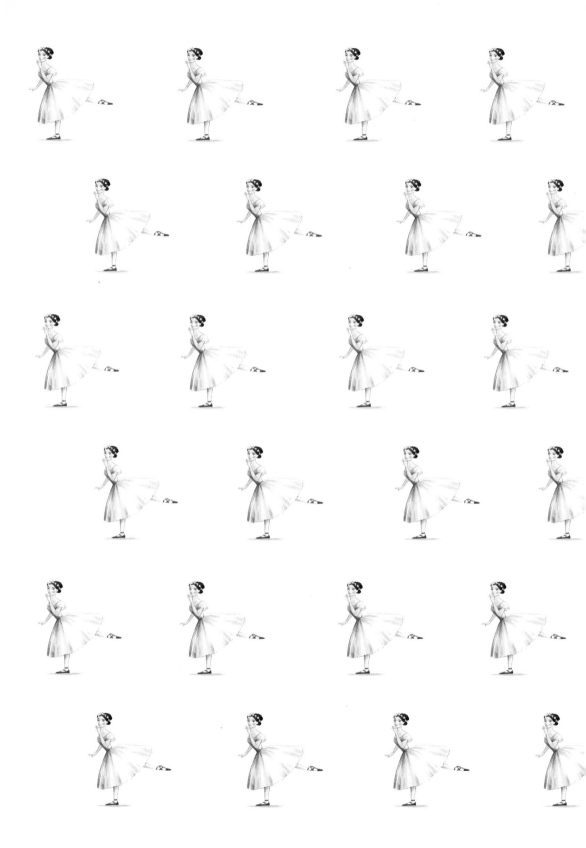